TREES OF THE TWENTIETH CENTURY
AND THE SHIP

Stephen Sturgeon

MADHAT PRESS
ASHEVILLE, NORTH CAROLINA

MadHat Press
MadHat Incorporated
PO Box 8364, Asheville, NC 28814

The Library of Congress has assigned
this edition a Control Number of
2015917319

ISBN 978-1-941196-23-6 (paperback)

Text by Stephen Sturgeon
Cover design and artwork by Marc Vincenz
Book design by MadHat Press

www.MadHat-Press.com

First Printing

Acknowledgments

Some of the poems in *Trees of the Twentieth Century* appeared in *Boston Review, The Charles River Journal, Dark Sky Magazine, Eyewear, Fulcrum: an Annual of Poetry and Aesthetics, Harp & Altar, Jacket, Open Letters Monthly, Tuesday; an Art Project* and *Typo*, and the collection was originally published by Dark Sky Books in 2011.

Portions of *The Ship* appeared in *The Battersea Review, elimae,* and *Petri Press*, and in 2014 Digraph Press published *The Ship* in a limited letterpress edition of eighty copies.

Many thanks to the editors who published my work.

CONTENTS

TREES OF THE TWENTIETH CENTURY

The Confabulators   5

Gourmand   9

Sunrise at Morning   10

Satan in Heaven   11

Thoughts of a Man   13

Cohoes Falls   16

La Ballade du phasme   17

Lines   18

Flyer for Joy Street   19

Out of Landis ~ Five Elegies

I.   Cassini Recalled   21

II.   The Clothes of Coronado   22

III.   Moustache   24

IV.   The Chronicles of Hugo Flake   25

V.   40 Years of Science   26

Why I Called   28

The Sailor's Head Held by a Tree (a fragment)   29

The Fountain   34

Kid Policeman   35

I Forget What You Say   36

1996 Snow Ball   37

In Pursuit of the Curtain Rod   40

To See No Light, and See   44

Parerga

i.   The Expulsion   45

ii. The Annunciation   46

iii. The Wizard   47

Bullroarer Ritardando   48

Love's Black Way   50

Originalia   51

360-Month Sundial   52

Forever in El Dorado   55

Epistola Cantabrigiensis   56

House with Paintings in It   59

THE SHIP

"I did not learn the passengers' names."   65

"We are in this boat."   66

"The letters I have written to the world"   67

"Days ago"   68

"To scoop water from the side"   69

"This river everyone I have met has fantasized"   70

"And it has become difficult to understand"   71

"New Year's Day must have come"   72

"I know the back of her hand like the bricks of Rome"   73

"Have you even married a mountain."   74

"The days are often faster"   75

"About a century ago the vocations"   76

"We in this boat entered a region"   77 "spinning spinning" 78

"Leave all this behind. Embark" 79

"The hole in the river bottom" 80

"Clip clip says the sky." 81

"Bastion of bombs sang" 82

"Pebbles crash out of the river" 83

"Rain walked down from the clouds" 84

"I rarely drink from my drinking glass." 85

"The river would fold into a wavy box" 86

"In exhaustion lives discovery." 87

"It makes little sense" 88

"One missed institution is a jail" 89

"I have narrated the betrothal of my will" 90

"The river's wings flap and articulate" 91

"the length of the world" 92

"Concerning the river's marriage," 93

"Nothing would tempt me" 94

"A scratching from beneath this boat" 95

"You will ask, now did this continue" 96

"Rivers supply the earth civilizations." 97

"Memory of a window" 98

"In my hands my eyes" 99

"In faith we held to the unswayable route" 100

About the Author 102

TREES OF THE
TWENTIETH CENTURY

to Matthew Spencer

There was once a great conflux of people in *Abdera*, a City of the Greeks, at the acting of the Tragedy of *Andromeda*, upon an extream hot day: whereupon, a great many of the spectators falling into Fevers, had this accident from the heat, and from the Tragedy together, that they did nothing but pronounce Iambiques, with the names of *Perseus* and *Andromeda*; which together with the Fever, was cured, by the comming on of Winter: And this madnesse was thought to proceed from the Passion imprinted by the Tragedy.

THOMAS HOBBES.

There is a point beyond which we must hold people responsible for accidents:

WYNDHAM LEWIS.

THE CONFABULATORS

Let us speak this time as if the loss
were retrievable. I speak to great birds,
coaxing their perch upon my burnt shoulders,
upon your hands loosing benedictions.
Oracles are not all predictable.
Let us too speak as they would yell to us,
flatly, of ghostes and spirites walkyng by nyght.

Shall I impart a rare secret, how great
famous conjurers, cunning men, ascend
by degrees to foretell secrets as they do?
The lessons teach beginner's thievery:
to deny derivation, to propel
the practice of memory to tomorrow
(*the future presentation of the past*),
and most importantly to make things fit,
and to throw flesh into the wold for dogs
unchained by flash itinerant wardens,
you splashing tracks wading the river's shore,
the run of gnash draining of threat far back.

I do not know the proper tone to take
mostly now and when the faces conjoin
expectant in cramped auditoriums
where piano music for left hand played
with right fist cracks, surrounds the night in flanks

of disappointment gleaned by both sides.
What do you speak after penguins enter
the trembling bear-baiting ring? Entrée trays
slide off laps onto the floor, the first act
takes back the stage to rehash. The English
is not a native tongue; still, you have no
second language to beg help. Speak error.

You'll fall safely and warm beside the stove
after the work has finished that long day.
Buenos dias, mon ami. All will right itself
in our honesty. These errors are correct.
They project a giant, marvelous light
by which a colder eye can study small
failures that veer lives off beyond; correct,
and cause us much of the (how do you say)
sweet joy; correct, in the light of honest
failure. Next door, the old girl can recall
when that street's name was changed from Strangler's Lane,
and that one from Embezzler's Ave., and one
by the bank from The Counterfeiter's Row.
All attempts to reclaim the swastika
have smoldered, despite our loose-handed stare
into the siren blast. That's contrition.

I'm stealing laughter from far in the dark.

O my gal—O my good good gal;
that's over; improvisation inspires
a thirst for theatrics more demonic
than the hawing of a mind's clipped blinking.
Drink a little water, Sylvie—a little
water now; that's over; only slavery
moulds song true. Maybe a man's name doesn't
matter that much; that's over; you can tell
a charlatan by the chalk whispering
out of his cuffs. What does it mean when things
present themselves; it means, it means that we
have seen them; that's over. That's over.

I trust that you have written me in. Your
made history rides a problematic
matrimony between what in the world
is real and honor to traditional
convenience. You honor all that you want,
forging and forgetting slick orbits
that bind our vows in transparent movements.
The motion to remove darkness from night
is an imposition worthy of Death.
Just forge my autograph to this warrant
and assume my attendance at the birth.

Mourning has levels to it, and we meet,
zipping different amplitudes in the shaft,
up down, sharing in transit a numb space.

Reclamation, as licentious as moon
steps; pairing wildflower to wallpaper.

GOURMAND

I tasted each inch of the earth.
I did not like it but I did it.
There were extravagant flavors,
Gobi, Horse Track, Lava Field, London ...

People saw a starving criminal
and mildly kicked me, or flicked me crumbs,
while I etched a new map of the world
inside my roving mouth.

Soon *Sweet*, *Acrid*, and their family failed.
When my tongue hardened it discovered
specimens of *No* persistent

everywhere. In the tang of sunrise
or populous night; on footprints, scurried;
stable, through the caterwauling clay: *No*.

Stephen Sturgeon

SUNRISE AT MORNING

The ground pursues us, we pursue the ground,
and my laugh is the laugh of the farmer's laugh,
laughing as the farmer grows the corn in his kitchen.
Or taking the switch to a ruddy stump,

one will say, "Does this move me? Am I a thought
betrayed?" And moving to a pot of husks
and dialing up the flame, there's no harm thinking,
"I put the smile on my creature's face.

I am more the more I move." But it is not the sun
prowling through Magellan's fortressed hair
that pulls, planet-like, thoughts into an ear.

This morning I have seen my creature die.
It is not the sun that makes, or can feel
the interminable burning of standing still.

SATAN IN HEAVEN

In the beginning I was happier.
The rocks spun. So close the air was to my face
I sparely breathed. It was a cold man
with thoughts like this:

there is no end to what was done.

Concludingly, I seethed, and found myself
among the savage environments,
enjoying it. No unresponsive censure
in the pit, nor gust nor plume where widows ran.

The clouds bore each other, anchored
to the deepest bowl of land,
and on the line they flailed. I said,
"Speak with me, I too am contained,"
and that was fine, I struggled with my smiles,
identifiable as they were,
though overwhelmed, and invisible.

Friends in this time of material and woe
were calamitous, spiteful, too deep below
to see what bellowed through my fears.

Enemies, by chance, were my only peers.
I watched them, from on a hill, at its top,
thinking, everything falls down that will come up.

Then, with the earth, my body twisted
as the memory of armies floating

Stephen Sturgeon

into the other scaled worlds like a worm.
And the water was full, and the fire
was full. Patches of grass curled into thoughts
festooning the multiple domes, physical,
eager to wreath creation's plangency
with a fiber that could perpetuate.

A shallow quarry grappled with its sand ...

I tore bushes entire from the ground
and tirelessly they fed within my hand.

THOUGHTS OF A MAN

I

Think of a man
arrayed on a beach

the force of the universe's
total light combined
and concentrated on his nose

His garments are the usual ones
He has no hope of abnormal wealth

nor hope to drift
one foot balanced on a pin
cushion across the Pacific

to great acclaim from the papers
Think of this man

of how his nose
should be his best feature

II

Returned from a far walk
through the Hungarian jungle
and having found success there
in our work

we thought about a man
You wait and I will tell you
Not your everyday character
Someone more like a water faucet

than is customary
He had priestly teeth
and a head like a carwash

When we began to think
of this man and his various ways
we had no more use for the world

III

Is it wrong
to think of a man
as one would think
of a girl

The needed energy

is enormous for this

Most advise against it
I do not see why

we should not think of men
as girls

think of men or as men
think of girls

I do not see
why we should think of men

COHOES FALLS

My dream was called "The Invention of Society
in Cohoes, NY," shale bed, parliament of paper mills

skidding ceremoniously into the Mohawk. To this day
my favorite vampire is the driveway of 24 Rose Court,

who scratched daily from onion-paper legs a tonic
to thwart woolen summer thirst. As you listen now

my voice can be discovered in gray icicles fanging
Bedford Street, which reliably congregate into the form

of a mastodon's skeleton, its wastewater translucence
like glassine. After cold fisticuffs when I was 8

with the chandelier, my mother dug crystal and wire
out of my hands, and dropped that garbage in an ashtray

while my conqueror slouched on the porch, drinking soup,
a rug draped on its baluster. Its knuckles had clinked "Our Town"

against my little nose. In another town minutes ago
I made 20 dollars on Sparks Street bumbling to my home,

because in the road I found it, and I make what I find.
You say what you hear, my house was called "Show Me the Way."

La Ballade du phasme

Black Moon snuck behind an Oriental screen.
Poor Miss Black Moon jitterbugs and unseen
spies occasion to whistle and unwind,
when her invitation is maligned.
When she falls, black moon sinks along the shine,

says What the world is this. Isn't mine.

Two black moons slouching, talking about bed,
sing blue-moon-I-knew-thee-when-you-were-red,

beseech of Old Black Moon What are you like?
A geyser. No. The Pine Barrens. A shrike
who eats my friend the walking-stick beneath a yew.
Black moon reflects I don't know what I'm like,
tho I'm cautious where I am. Too true, too true.

LINES

speaking of judgments
of value and recompense
we might speak of lightning
what vaults from the ground
to electrocute a cloud
or sinks from cloud to ground

and which of these is better
respite for the wicked
or for the merely damned

when nothing is wasted
like when the sink drinks
water your glass missed
or you leave the radio playing
in the room and animals
listen to what you can't

FLYER FOR JOY STREET

This self-indulgence has not left me.
Normal relations seem mild.

i

Ride on the T all day for three days
reading the seminarian's guidebook
Cultural Affairs in Boston.

People start to wonder what's
really going on. "Do I belong here"
they think at the Maverick station

"I just want to see the octopus
at the New England Aquarium."

ii

John Wieners kept an octopus.
He had it in his piano.

The one way he could sleep
was by listening to his persuasion

tying it trapped. String by string
the music snapped and the joints

that latched the words together.
"There goes another sinister"

from the train you'll see the hospital
"solitudinarian faceless past me."

iii

How like the color of magazines
his hair. The advert glaze and wet-thumbed ink.
Now on every fence spike, a strand,
on each gas slick in the Charles and the fingers
of unrepeatable people. You trade handshakes.
They disappear.

iv

Professionally in the bulrushes a violin sounds Auld Lang Syne,
Kidnap requests spin across the dial of AM radio
But for friends enough and hotels any poem is obtainable
The night stops with the questions what is left and who has it

OUT OF LANDIS
FIVE ELEGIES FOR LANDIS SAVAGE EVERSON (1926–2007)

I

CASSINI RECALLED

Something lost in the ciborium amazing
in transit; bled to zero promise
at leucotomy's shunt and withdrawal;

digested by the forgiven's demands
for enriched conduct. In theory,
Forgetting Medicine permits living again

fresh visions of our satellites stretching
threads of descent. Water near ailing Saturn
could spout from glacial Oceans of Youth,

so much Lethe-wash, hell in the neighborhood.
It is midnight and all's well.
Brothers and sisters go wandering,

what last thing that won't come back—
an ice reef can nourish mouths of its temper—
what paucity of ruth to second grief.

II

The Clothes of Coronado

An overcoat, red shoes, red bag.
These are the clothes I talk to
in my kitchen on a different coast.
Sometimes the view into my garden
is dim, and I juggle the phone
listening to whatever time there is,
the past, the future.

Each lace leads on to a button,
a fly, a pipe tucked into a hole.
A dash of string alone will be seen,
flying from my head, off an ocean cliff.
Stop thinking about coming here
and tell me more about what you wear.

It's hard to see into my garden
where the fence has been lovingly chewed,
so I write out a good-bye letter.
There is a collection of hats in a bin
in my garage that you should have
and the handle needs grease.
The fur coats have fleas.
Have you ever been out west with me,
counting the basements I laid?

I left a shirt in every one of them.
If I had them now, the pockets
would be filled with telephones

ringing the pants my friends really lost.
They made me do it, name all the clothes
that walked straight into your home.

III

MOUSTACHE

A guy comes to you and says "The pages
in my book are like rabbits, hiding

when they should hurry, late. I haven't
had a birthday in two years." Your head hears

how far his moustache stoops to duck words.
So all things now do speak his face

and the streetlamps gush its last remains.
Where did the moustache learn that tune?

 "I grew my moustache to feel more
like a rabbit, whose whiskers tell him

where to go. I want to know where
to go." You want him to shut his mouth

about rabbits, want to kiss his moustache
instead of watching it always grow.

 "Your skin needs more fur, then I'd stay and laugh
with you, at the alphabet and ghouls,

but the dream radiates its own problems.
And one of them is you."

IV

THE CHRONICLES OF HUGO FLAKE

In my bed I encounter cannibals
but this skin has been reserved for another.
It is a duty to laugh through the deranged
season God has set working. Friends are here,
I know; to visit whom, I do not.

All has changed to foreigners' food. Once more
I consider the pedigree of time,
and see no puzzle to its address.
The fronds in my photo have long been yours.
Wastrel, you have found me.

V

40 Years of Science

What one astronaut says to another
is heaven's business, communicable
by fusion and frisson alone. Orbit

had been vicious to their visions. Timeless
protons and propaganda had melted
the re-entry shield. Once a week they learned

how, despite machinery's schadenfreude,
love can transmit in outer space: keenly,
while audio from their families played,

they would display gazes, listening
to earth but watching each other, like beasts.
"You were going to tell me something else,"

or "When we sleep, still I dream about space,
one dazed night reaching past our world. We, though,
are here, and have done that"—besides these

there was no truth to say. On walks outside
their brittle capsule, they went holding hands,
feverish, memorizing through visors

blacknesses that did and did not surround.
Climbing into their circular quarters,
de-suiting and trading turns with the comb,

memories no longer complained. Humid
from breath, now they nap. The solar system
uses gravity's surreal transactions

for deadweight, tips its discs and clustered chips
observably away from live sightlines.
Even so, the universe is a grave.

Why I Called

I bought a bag of food

I took it home and put it on the table

It moved and flipped over

I looked at it

I opened it

My dead friend's hand came out

I said hello

It wriggled its fingers at me

I said how are you

It gave me the thumbs up sign

I said what do you want

It pretended to write

I brought it pencil and paper

It wrote down your phone number

I called you

The Sailor's Head Held by a Tree

(a fragment)

> *In any case the whole drift of social development was to make
> things difficult for the independent minstrels and to restrict the
> area of their wanderings.*
>
> E. K. CHAMBERS, The Medieval Stage

I

It was not time to cheer the day.
A sailor's head sat in a tree
preaching on what it could not be.

"You must have come from striking far
to spread your country's ideas here."
"That is not why. It was not far."

"Then you have taken to that tree
to witness our philosophy."
"I did not do it. I can't see."

II

A child behind his tented hands.
An empty house someone commands.
Such quiet thrived in that tree's bends,

it could be why the head came there—
to fixate a shambolic fear.
It is not why. It cannot hear.

It hears the calm that comes before
and after closings of a door.
It hears the dawn throughout the day.

III

Almost, almost the head began.
The tree was too live, or too wan.
The head's eyes, a constellation,

would weep, like starlight through a sieve.
Some wanted this pale head to leave.
"Explain to us if you're alive."

"But things I say will not remain
equal to their naïve demesne.
What you don't see, I hear the same."

IV

"I think he wants to sail the land,
and rub his keel where waters end,
to feel different, and understand."

"I think no matter where he goes,
if he arrives then he is lost.
Absence, to him, is a caress."

"With every word, my final bow.
The moon erodes. The breezes flow.
I will become what I am now."

V

Now when it rained the head would stare,
regard each drop, pronounce each fair,
and drink some with paternal care.

And when it snowed the head would sing,
aware of how the cold flakes clung
and wilted like subjects to king.

It sang like mowers to a rose
in error they drowsily thresh,
who, sorry, hear sound, and not voice.

VI

The head was offered fish, then wine,
a veal-calf roasted in the sun,
and apples, and refused to dine.

"He will not eat because no mouth
responds to banquets after drought.
Our meals arrive too soon, too late."

"Hunger aspires to be pain.
I want no food. I am my own.
A stone well nourishes a stone."

VII

"You're only 'lost' for just so long.
Some ages pass, you become 'gone.' "
The people came, people walked on.

"I can't remember who they were,
counting leagues until the dry shore,
the buildings' shades each one would bear—"

the sailor's head searched its wet thought.
"Ideas are nowhere in my art ...
The sun is cold ... The stars are not ... "

VIII

Concerning years, how they black out
to loose and perpetual sight
that frees the witness to his doubt,

engraves imprimaturs on thaw:
those unseeing—oh, how they saw
the dumb reflections of an hour

initiate the head's prelude,
on solace tangled in the word;
on constancy; on ash renewed.

Stephen Sturgeon

THE FOUNTAIN

to Katia Kapovich

Remember the greasy park
on the final warm day of that hot year—

pigeons that pouted toward the curbs
with a bench-woman feeling her torn teeth
as if each were a son banished from distances
paltry with age—

what were you doing posing
inside its drained fountain while a bus
struck past the cabbage-green fence
bleating at heaven and hell? Later the rain

stuck on our skins like candles' gelatinous wax
and wiping it from my arms with newspaper
closing my eyes I could not see you

in your spotted shorts stepping into that bowl,
then, sanely glancing at the traffic's maze,
tying your hair back with an elastic
the way a climber will do
before catching onto the mountain.

KID POLICEMAN

to Sophia Nikolayev

It's time to think about the kid
policeman. He's short as a lamb,
and unveils his cratered body
only to the question of sleep

from a glow-vest. His glowing
vest drags against the face that rules
traffic. When he's hit, he gets up
and spits into the galaxy.

Not lazy, not needful of guests
telling him his job, the noontime
breaks into morning, falls under
spells, and reawakes as homework.

The parade of age, the children
walking up. Every street has mice.
Every lamb dozes in the road.
Every cop wishes he's a kid.

I FORGET WHAT YOU SAY

Beg for rest but real rest is work,
strong work. Pretend to know homelessness
and death to a fault, and talk about it,
because you've been homeless, because you've died.
Flutter at reconcilers' screens like paper
boys scrape paper girls' storm windows,
like a beggar. Consider this friendship
amongst masked parties—"Your pseudonymous
confidante"—siblings shouting tree to tree.

The sealine mumbles up its binges,
scraps of a yellow wall bed down
with shells corroding on a wreck of shoals.
The mouth's calling is all deconfession,
though the last thing never comes back. Tell me
about the time you dialed M for me.

1996 SNOW BALL

I

She completely grasped her chance
for balance.
Stepping into the Christmas weather
of their juvenile village,

she was a work of flagrance, crystal
reflecting the moment of its reflection;
he and she were like a new creation
from a revisionary model of mind,

look anywhere you want.
Shod for the gym dance
she and he resemble shacks,

you do not know what is in them.
You do not look.
You do not know where you are.

II

Look anywhere you want,
each twirl conspicuous
in empirical failure
but sustaining well this daughter.

He like a wall built
from the remains of sixteen
previous walls,
for his life there's a light bulb a trash can a

medium sized railroad spike a mirror
with goldflake fringe a chair with bone
inlay a safety switch a fire ax,

and "I have banned such plan
as would commemorate her entry
unless she trail a train of shell"

III

Hung up his hat and
plucked at his tooth
on an unequivocal ampersand
left over in her kissing booth

They had to get used to America
though they were the ones born there.
They clacked fingernails
and left shoeprints in the hallway water

and left each other.
No emblem assigned them.
Charcoal nylons

desperately sketched will not do.
Come into the garden-city, love
Come away, come away

Stephen Sturgeon

IN PURSUIT OF THE CURTAIN ROD

A man tracked a curtain rod that blazed through a forest,
and as he furiously traveled, with him there went

the hair of Jesus' head inching along,
a river of skulls a black girl swam,
bells in the sun at cascade and ring,
tallow swept up from a fast-burning palm,
Britain's crown jewels stitching one hundred shirt collars,
moldering tree stumps that suckled a boy,
philosophical plants strapped under root cellars,
our dream's last rest batted to scraps as a toy,
Magdalene's glance at the petulant sky,
communities of mirrors, flush in séance,
blacksmiths joining the ends of barn hay,
the trial of youth hidden under long pants,
Lucifer's fingers on the strings of our harm,
conciliatory pause adjudicating blame,
and the mane of the lion flashing after the lamb,

however the night was calm.
However the night was, the night was calm

in the screeching air tearing the road
walked in pursuit of the curtain rod.

As the man followed the rushing curtain rod,
he lingered for danger, and on the way the noise

of tremulous cyclones falling through a shirtsleeve,
an orchestra that entered a whiskey decanter,
the many-times dead at reluctance to grieve,
pillows' suffocation and harlequins' banter,
mariachi jousting the knights of the table,
a box alone adrift along floor edges and black stairs,
gunshots mastering the art of the fable,
Houdini, who lapped the scurf from his sores,
all vacant nooses complaining for work,
belligerent men at high mass on all-fours,
the hip-bone of God splintering a wrecked hulk,
leaded glass mottled grey at the centers of spires—
made its way to the hunting man alien from home,
ignorant of what now could be his name
and tired with dragging his frame on the loam,

however the night was calm.
However the night was, the night was calm

over the weeds, the dirt, and the sod
destroyed in the wake of the curtain rod.

When the man had gotten close to gaining the curtain rod,
he looked through the forest's branches, and he saw

a fearless blank ocean recoiling from snow,
heavenly junkyards where cherubs built trash,
gentlemen smoking with nothing to show,
the taste of the hairpin, the glow of the lash,

a baker who butchered the whim of his ache,
the Celestial Rail-road biting its tail,
last century's comedy cork-smeared in black,
the art of involuntary failure and fall,
infants destroying the roof of the moon,
dice tumbling over the shine of a blade,
peripheral ladyship poured into a gown,
children loping to bed, and they were afraid,
the beast of the air with the beast of the stream,
what each man kills, the soul of his flame,
and bank vault doors locking in frosted foam,

however the night was calm.
However the night was, the night was calm

for the man so fearful to look by his side,
pedaling his feet toward the curtain rod.

When the curtain rod had at last become unreachable,
the man walked still, and as he walked he knew

how the graces of us close up dark like umbrellas,
that these old things are about to get thrown away,
how the scales of our grievance sink down lithe endeavors,
the thing you will hear is the thing you must say,
where cauldrons roast nightly the lover will look,
there will be one if by land and three if by grave,
when heaven imploded the earth only shook,
we lie down in our cities and wake up in a cave,

to drink all its poison a throat should be young,
courage looks back at its deserts of salt,
the person who sings will not go unsung,
who fought in the fields, those here, also, fought:
the angel of ditches and the demon of chrome;
a mouth on the ground whose tongue, forced, struck a drum;
pencil-men; bathers; sea-sailors; in them all, a hymn;

however the night was calm.
However the night was, the night was calm

on the path that holds ever the scorch of the flood
laid in the prints of the swift curtain rod.

Stephen Sturgeon

To See No Light, and See

Time was, I could get a rise out of you.
Where have I known you? Songsters known to say
longevity's pre-empted—it's gonged off,
or it's sung ritualistically wrong—say
Get used to nothing that does not use you.
Wisdom for ages owns us. I'd have you
believe that most intercessory prayer
is negative thinking, that its power
cannot save so much as prolong a life,
but I'd have you do so much. Check out this
power: sparrows have devoured my palms.
Retrieve your green eyes from the crystal dish.
Unsew your ears. There are truer wonders.
Salutes. Flag ceremonies. No, let us
not speak. Smoke-signals. Memory. *I'll pass.*

PARERGA

I

THE EXPULSION

Cannot translate angelic malfeasance
into the precursor to a prayer
or find words in the God-damned fields and trees.
They wanted what could not be found or worked for
and having exhausted weariness
of its élan, the self-wounding self
rewound tottered like a pinetop
in the gale or above the ax.
What harms we carry see us through
to harms we cannot,

cannot budge now past the intelligence
in the final outlaster, maker
of manner and silence shaking in mouths.
Only, to waddle while the slow land
filters the day ... Some tears drip to the ground.
It is hard to be rid of them, the perfect
anagram of themselves, spun
within hours of their nebulous
originals, all-expanding, going
and coming, coming and going after all.

II

The Annunciation

Everything was OK until the day she woke
with the lights, and the field swayed to the right
so the stalks reclined like the dying,
marooned. It was then that this story began
which cannot be related, the Feast
of Radiant Lips, such forthrightness
under a clogging sky ... Truly
you can count nothing against this
when the last things have been arranged
into their misericord, though many will try.

It was (so it was) an angel's doing. It was
the angel who came here, an angel
who spoke then. What one eye banishes
the other eye must see. It was an angel
who forfeited our remaining
breaths. Not that we should know
innocence passed by, which cannot be related.
Away in the breath, the jury
of her reluctance hid, in breath action
should resound. Though this too is not the way.

III

THE WIZARD

A few people lifted their heads, the blind first.
DANILO KIŠ, "Simon Magus"

The third thing I did was pummel through clouds
when the air buckled like a rotted knee
beneath my sandals. I thought I'd forgotten
how to float, but soon knew it was not I
who had risen me like a broken toy
to the carpenter's lens, countless miles.
Thereafter all was wind—at one moment
I even flapped my arms ... The first thing was
not difficult, shaman's rhetoric, my
cold eyes cast into the cold crowd, and they,

such people, latched their taunts onto my trick
which even I had thought impossible.
The second thing was to accept myself
as divine: I watched the earth's scope broaden
until those peasants' screams fell short of me;
I turned around and around, protected
in the sky's immutability; I
wept at the grace of this action, and felt
the magnanimity of centered words.
I did not see it belonged to someone else.

BULLROARER RITARDANDO

i

Breaking through the wheat
beyond austere Appalachia

a buffalo shone his horned teeth
at the previous hour enfaced on his eyes

and it was a sullen noise.
It was the wheat's hour.

ii

Beyond the wheat the previous hour
waited for Appalachia to rise.

Beyond Appalachia the buffalo
rolled in the wheat.

In the wheat where the eye was beaten tan
the eyes were girded tight and round.

iii

Hallelujah buffalo! Appalachia cried.
Without a witness but its sound

the robust sullen wheat expires.
Roaring rolling in provender

the previous hour leaves the eyes.
The buffalo leaves his skin behind.

Stephen Sturgeon

Love's Black Way

All things decay
& so must our sleigh

H. D. THOREAU

A bush lit our final night
with the sled. I'd found a small
lane, and faraway a piece
of gold. There were other people
too there. And someone said she thought
we were very old, for a damp
to crawl upon like oiled sheets.
Going sledding now and never again.

In the bush hips creaked like a ship.
Our new coats twisted. To sled
here and there cornered but spry
through wild passages, to relive
at any time rescinded faith
or manners. The call was let. Barks
steamed. Truthfully the woods forget
all the ideas this friendship had.

ORIGINALIA

Perpetual house of the fled,
August's swarms ushered you with squalls
of rain-scrapped leaves raining on pails,
hot scrimmages laid down in mud.

The mineral soap and bread for dawn.
A kettle bristles on its seat
composing breath, the sun's terrain
blanching onto clouds its secret:

the girl watched her brother buckle
his waist, sniff in the mirror's blast,
at last descend to milk and crust.

360-Month Sundial

March 1980

The naming of names is a redoubtable thing.
It begins with a name. Take this apple.
It has no name, will never be named. But
many things grow named ... They grew for ages

before the names,
and will know more before they stop. Or cities:
Las Vegas, Los Angeles. What should I say?
My child, my child ...

Or books: *The Histories, The Plays.*
The name of the next book will be *Fluid
Exchanges* and *The History*

of Natural Mystery.
As a concept, the universe laughs.
There is no "why" there.

NOVEMBER 1986

In my dreams of women, D'Annunzio
figures sometimes, at other times Billy Wilder,
as the females step in and out of cars,

masking their faces from the sun or rain,
flipping an egg in the pan, smiling
at doctors on whom their well-being depends.

And off, in the basement, my name
meddles with a pump, sweating, refreshing light bulbs.

I have written my name on everything I could find;
the objects wear and the signature stands alone.

FEBRUARY 1992

The world ends, and we listen. Every sound
is the sound of the world ending, though we
never hear everything ...
... and I listen in every way to the one who is not there.
My child, my child,

I am the best worker, but abstain most months.
You may witness me heartily at work
from moment to moment daily.
The product of my infrequent employment
is sustained illusion.

OCTOBER 2004

The wealth of world has not been distinguished
from our forbears, the first seers,
the little people who were likely blue or loud.

It is good to pass by a brook,
with so much reasoning behind your brow,
so much distinction between footprints in the swamps.

I am not grateful for the usual things. As always,
I have taken my stand in a puddle of brains.

MARCH 2010

I want to see the bed, not mine.
The bed of the absent laugher,
of nearly disputed vacancy.
What is left is to speak.

That is not left me.
Perpetual minstrelsy at stake,
forbearance of further innuendo.
No name, as good as any name.

FOREVER IN EL DORADO

Caligula in catacombs journeyed like a forlorn claw
but his laughs leapt into aqueducts, sewers, acres of corn,

and mattresses I inhabited underneath ledges
at age 3, tranq'd into dysphonic phantomhood. For thirty years

my best friend was a bolt of lightning. He would visit me
nightly and speak of America, the stars disinterring

their cores, turmoil building up mangled valleys, swarming
to whirlpools, long awaiting, swirling an incandescent end—

still I would gather the latency of relatives' crude
and diminished eyes while managing my fat empires

from a grotty telephone booth hidden in grape vines
on the corner of Vliet and Garner. Courage, lightning bolt,

for the purposeless circuitry of my race. Go and see
that guillotine who plays the lute in my parents' bedroom

so sweetly it could put to a rest a frost-frayed and thorny
whippoorwill crashed in a sand-patch, nubbed beak squealing,
        the eyes

a carnival of threats, one wing that could slice through a knotty
cloud and leave the rest behind. There is nothing, nothing.

EPISTOLA CANTABRIGIENSIS
(OVER AN OLD COPY OF *ENEMIES OF PROMISE*)

I thought I saw you on Arrow Street, rippling
like an infant scarecrow's burnt-orange rags
or tight in a green-striped sailor's shirt, cocking
your head side to side against the tearing flyers
stapled onto any wooden things. I may have been unawake,

holding an imaginary and heavy orb in my hand,
because nothing rests there. I do not think so.
Going between two places, I never want to arrive,
and would rather go on perpetually a passenger, passing
through spicy air and scenes of acquaintances spatting,
whose fight, though meaningless, is the only thing.
Or, it would mean as much as anything else,
your alien capacity to void senescence,
my ripped shoes welcoming the mud. Constantly there is this
            motor
running itself nearly to cataclysm around my ears.

The fact of ears reminds one so deliriously of death, eventualities
come to look the same, parallel lines that meet the way
a pair of hands does, clapping out of the nightmare.
Why should there be a place to go?
Thinking about the UCL variants for *The Princess*,
I know it is a world of hollow shows;
thinking about Dublin I know this life
is a warm fullblooded life; and I am happy to say
more than ever these have been pitted in a long bout
where neither wins, and they come to exist simultaneously
inside each other, like Balthus and Hogarth—

there is nothing more important than the spot of weakness
that makes good things work. A hatch-door hinge opens
a basement where aquariums splashing with bright fish
are found alongside a poster of Marilyn Monroe
touching her footsole to her knee. You know these,
remember them, tying your white V-neck to the Maple trunk
across the street, leaving, and leaving the rest to the city.

City buses are crashing
and I can't hear Murray Perahia. That is part of the ordeal,
having to make up sounds for the music
that sputters beneath melee, and making the two
play inside each other, like the pictures before,
like Marilyn and the fish, like your field rags and sailor-suit.
What a pain in the neck for people who need to be amazed
and need to keep the electricity paid. Isn't it enough
that Lame Duck Books is closing down? *Talk with old friends*
is the most pleasant and least enlightening kind of dialogue.
The contours of their minds are already familiar, a well-known scene
which one accepts and loves. Erasmus would erase us.

And standing in front of the Cummings house you can't see
        anything.
A big grey fence and pines that were not growing
when Estlin was growing and drooling rhymes
about elephants, which his mother folded away
as if they had been funeral lilies or Easter cards.
They did a fine job of work killing all the old things
we'd like to see now, I suppose in the 60s and 70s
when old things were popularly bad and everyone believed

they were going mad, and they wrote about nothing else,
though they were wrong. Squinting, one might conjure
Scofield Thayer breaking his head on the slats,
crazing after his abducted and indifferent wife.

I don't care that life will end in an explosion of guilt and cancer.
Criticism is rarely not for clowns. Things I want are against the
        law.
To accommodate the drifting particulars, the unexpected sense
piping out of dead buildings and ruined families, there will be
another strain of this science to learn. As luck will have it,
there will not be a place to go. For the moment
on Arrow Street I thought I saw you. The day was about travel,
guideless and apparent, and the hour-bells struck until no time
        was left.

HOUSE WITH PAINTINGS IN IT

The end he wanted was always elsewhere.
He had not introduced the brightnesses
that would not leave or help him off the boards

when he needed to rise or sit alone,
but they stayed, yawning in his yawning eyes.
He could not participate for their mirth

and conceived of funiculars arrayed
on verdigris slopes wet by eastern spring,
stationed throughout auspicious altitudes,

early as he hanged pictures on the wall.
But they did not assemble how he would.
Humble at mirrors, often travesties

in craquelure seemed there, and a doctor
splaying the convalescence in his hands,
hands like the homely colors men would hold

when they scan pigeons cringing to an eave.
But there were never pigeons, never eaves.
The tree beats the window, and he is flayed

to see the caustic colors assemble,
the beauty of showing up hours late,
a kind of courage in not beginning.

THE SHIP

to Alison Walsh

Of these things no recorder;

    …

For one is beat with blasting tears,
    And burned with raging weather,
And reapt in fiery haste—, the ears
    Half-ripe, dead-ripe, or neither:

    …

Why, for some peep of meaning clear,
    Should we ourselves deliver
Up to the stream, which even here
    Roars past us like a River?

FREDERICK GODDARD TUCKERMAN.

I did not learn the passengers' names.
I may have learned them but in the way
that one does not learn the learned thing
But the name of the river and of its ministry
I learned

We are in this boat.
We know the colors of heaven and hell.

I ripped off some hair
to throw into the wind.

Our injuries are not unique
in that they are disgraceful.

It is usual to conclude this is punishment
Punishment in paradise

The letters I have written to the world
while traveling in this boat
contain the same message more often than not
The world is terrifying
and this boat is not much better
but it is better.

Days ago
by this time it may have been months
those of us in this boat
passed by a site of sacrifice

A column's capital
tipped from its place
rolled into the river's water

By all appearances
it is hunting us

Worse than this
the water is talking

To scoop water from the side
of this boat and look inside it.
Too many found distant faces or futures
inside the water they scooped
from the side of this boat.

This river everyone I have met has fantasized
and dreamed of as monster, mother, saint,
at least I have seen this river
though from the crouch of a stagehand.

In my time in this boat I have looked down
and no longer do I think answers
should be composed
to questions

It is becoming clear to me
one may construct a house out of the river.

And it has become difficult to understand
what of our thoughts has been provided
by the river's stalking voice. And we are in fear.
Our actions will not be ours when we are called.
Looking last night into the core of the sky
I saw my wailing mother.

New Year's Day must have come
It may have been that dismal day
we expounded on the rudder.

We screamed and shook hands,
the next day woke up

We are in this boat,
millions of people
it must
be

a vacuum

I know the back of her hand like the bricks of Rome
but she vanishes into the glutted throng
and when she returns I do not recognize
her or the bricks of her hand, my cathedral.

Her tears you would see on book jackets. The river
floats trade winds to no vector, the commerce
a river must imagine is its heraldic right
skitters for hammocks slung in men and women's minds.

Hold to the river. The wind's force does not betray
how destination is cradled in God's mouth
now frowning now smiling at time's invisibility

licking the hull of this boat. My cathedral
city knocking against her own ears' doorbells
has its place and vanishes and I do not recognize.

Have you even married a mountain.

Have you even loved a river or lake
visited it
and married it.

The days are often faster
than the transit of the sun.
They drown into night before the regal sun
has finished its routine.

In this boat
transactions
are between the eyes and the water.

About a century ago the vocations
of educated men and ladies
allowed for long absences from society
and this time would be spent on boats.

We in this boat entered a region
where groves of trees made of water
grew out of the river's water.
A child among us jumped
into a water-tree's wet leaves
and scampered through its flowing branches.

spinning spinning
we in this substantial
dialogue with creation
or the unassuming vitriol
of a creator's whimsy
and flashing dance

Leave all this behind. Embark
today for any past clue helpful
that will reveal the clandestine fortitude
of the river's indomitable current.

The hole in the river bottom
takes in water like a drain
and the other hole in the river bottom
pours water into the river.

It is like a brain,
so much of the same thing
going in and out at every moment.

Clip clip says the sky.
What is that noise.
No one knows.

Fisk fisk say the trees.
Theories of an eventual waterfall

circulate among the drastic people.
I have my own theories.
Theories of a human waterfall.

Bastion of bombs sang
The peripatetic Boomerang
Someone now here in this boat
will not stop thinking

The moths come out and frisk in hair
Is it true they are souls
As I transition into moth-hood
will it be fear or delight I feel for flight

Unwelcome answers
The coast of Australia heaped with questions
Have we been shackled in lieu of shackles
Does elegance have a place
in this boat
When the river ceases to speak
does it listen
What madman would have the river listen

Pebbles crash out of the river
and into this boat.
Some have never stepped foot
into this boat
bouncing like a screwball metronome
on the drunken water

Rain walked down from the clouds
into our opening and closing mouths
in the figure of numerous sluices
operated by an incompetent lunatic.

Before long many spoke up
wanting a government to take account
chiefly of the unimaginable sounds.

I rarely drink from my drinking glass.
Instead on days I think I have found God
I fill it with water from the river
and empty my drinking glass on my head.

It may be a single day in which this is happening
a day with thousands of days and nights inside it
nevertheless a day

The river would fold into a wavy box
and levitate miles into the sky.
We would reach at the peaks below us
watching the snow on these infrequent days.

Were they the sum of our joys
the journey in this boat like a canoe
would be palatable
but so many joys deride us.

In exhaustion lives discovery.
And the river resembles exhaustion.
The river ran in iodine
People brandished their blades
in cavalier fashions
Can you bear to see
what will be achieved
after the hour of exhaustion
The river reflects the trees
but the river does not reflect
this boat or we who ride it.
For now, I am, and this river is,
a traveler many times disassembled
that collects itself. When the collection fails
that day will mark the new kingdom

It makes little sense
what the river says when it talks

Turn Back Turn Back
No Forge Ahead Forge Ahead
You Can Do Neither

What the river says
makes less sense
when it does not talk

The Belly of a Roof
Conceals the Grave and the Secret
of the Eternal Life You will not Experience
though Eternally You Excavate the Roof

One missed institution is a jail
where the unlikeable would live.

I have narrated the betrothal of my will
and the arrangement has embellished me senseless.
Fire plays inside the unplumbed trees.
This boat takes part in that game.

Nothing has been built to navigate
a boat like this into our sensations.
This may be Sumatra.
I cannot fathom the fathomable.

The river's wings flap and articulate
what a person hears exiting the Hippodrome,
the cascade of crowds and rubbings of shoes
as the sky pours hail and the earth creaks open.

So the river flies off leaving behind this boat
that goes on in confounded ways

the length of the world
its terror uniform

into what
inscrutable
talons
they flee

to spectate an eternal operation
through and through of pristine chance

imponderable voyage
pity pity

Concerning the river's marriage,
it calmed the excitable animals
into long sleep, in which they produced
tears the color of equatorial fruit,
and it was called a successful marriage.

Nothing would tempt me
to explain what residence on such a craft
as this could matter

broken anchor
soaking material

is it love
grasping the weed bed
on the river's bottom
and her feet trail behind her in the current
and the weed roots unsheathe
and love grabs a fresh weed
and water pushes past her eyes

A scratching from beneath this boat
no longer unsettles us
though it persist for what we count as miles.

As pilgrims we accept the trivial
unmaskings of the earth's unknowableness.

If you have the seen the lights
turning on and off in an empty lot
where a magnificent house used to stand

your mind has begun its marination
for this meal, or if you have imagined
the window's air to be of ocean birth.

You will ask, now did this continue
Did this continue how a wire continues
to feed on the storm's lightning

Yes that is how it continued

You will ask, did this end fitfully
the way a man would walk
as for the first time he walked

It went on this way until it did not

Rivers supply the earth civilizations.
Lately we have been introduced
to the point that we had not been civilized
and the river is civilizing us.

Memory of a window
In this boat there is no window
The destinations I would delay
to see a window

Through the window I would imagine air
from the top of water climbing in
clapping my arm and finding me distinct
from the limitless other bearers of windows

and evening would continue
sights of friends standing in the trees outside
blowing their sanction onto my activity
stormed up and perpetrated far from hoax

for the window was my friend

Window window falling fast

In my hands my eyes

I admit I eventually took out my eyes.

held them a cantankerous moment
and cast them into the river
hoping to see what was there
and if indeed there was something
in the caverns constantly at work
diligently creating

And in demented darkness
I rose into a demented sleep

My eyes were back
when I awoke

carrying the outrageous memory
of the actions blistering beneath this boat
that I remember
it is foolish to communicate.

In faith we held to the unswayable route
with this boat twining reality
and at that we were honored

even as another future
guarded its events
in all the moments this boat threaded.

For who of us would be cursed to evaluate
milk clambering from the rock's cleft.

I am a young animal
tearing away at life.

MAY 23, 2010
BUFFALO, NEW YORK

Stephen Sturgeon

About the Author

STEPHEN STURGEON was the Editor of *Fulcrum: an Annual of Poetry and Aesthetics* from 2006 to 2011. He is the English and American Literature Librarian at the University of Iowa.

Lightning Source UK Ltd.
Milton Keynes UK
UKHW040700300622
405186UK00001B/81